Dedication

The book is firstly dedicated to my lovely wife, Maritza, my son James Jr., my daughter, Saunteena and the new addition to my family, Semaj.

My mother Louise deserves a hug and a kiss for her unconditional support.

I dedicate the bulk of this book to the young people who has it so rough for so many reasons. I pray that a poem or two will inspire you.

I wrote many poems to the youth. Some poems encourages them to speak or accept the truth.

I didn't need to arrange a letter... We can all change to make the world better.

This work is also dedicated to all the formal educational institutions that have educated me. The institutions includes The Boston Public Schools, Northeastern University, Northeastern University Law School and Cambridge College.

The informal educational settings includes the family, church and community.

Acknowledgement

Firstly, I give God the thanks and praise for engaging me with his love and wisdom.

I want to publicly thank my family members (they know who they are) who encouraged me to "Go for it."

Special thanks to Ruthanne Bracey who from the start has been my listening ear. Thank You!

Thank you Sandra of Johnson Enterprises... You did it again!

Lastly, but most personally, I want to thank my lovely wife, Maritza for supporting all that I do. To her I would like to offer the following poem:

*****

A Letter to My Wife

Dear Maritza,

Thank you for sticking with me
Through thick and thin...
You've helped me in so many ways,
To count them, I don't know
Where I would begin.

You've supported all my new ideas
You sat attentive and showed me you
Care...

No one else could compare to you
No one else could support me
The way you do.

You've given me love, support
And understanding from the start
For all that, *I love you*
From the bottom of my heart.

Introduction

Thinking aloud is allowed. How appropriate the title. This book provides a platform for me to express what is on my mind and allows me to educate at the same time.

Many of these poems were derived from real life experiences that have happened to me. Some ordeals do in fact continue and will perhaps persist until the spirit of love and truth invades and occupies all hearts involved.

The comfort I get in sharing these is that the message is the unadulterated truth. Oftentimes the truth hurts but the appreciation for the truth can provide comfort and healing.

Because what is said is the truth, I make no apologies. For if I apologize for the truth, I would in essence condone a lie. That would be a real problem because too many lies are what got our society in the situation it is in.

Further, not enough of us who know the truth will speak the truth, never mind act.

The first step to changing our world for the better is to think about it. So for beginners: "Thinking Aloud is Allowed."

Contents

Baby

Community Awareness

Dedication

Friendship

General

Inspiration

Love

Personal

Religious

R.S.V.P.

Dear Mommy,

I thank God, you, and daddy for my
Creation...Not knowing exactly when I'm
Coming, you must be whacked with
Anticipation.

Who would think that I would have a nine
Month invitation...And poor you had to take all
That medication...Soon you'll be calling the
Ambulance, fire department or the police
Station.

And of course, they'll ask for all kinds of
Information...And anxious daddy is probably in
A *corner*, somewhere engaged in meditation.

Nevertheless, when I come out you can forget
About taking that well deserved vacation!

Special Delivery

*Doctor, doctor, please take me out...When you do,
I just might shout! My mom will be glad and
That's no doubt.*

*For her, no more pain...Especially when blood is
Taken from the vein.*

*Doctor, doctor, please add my name to your file...
My mom is anxious to greet me with a smile.*

*Make room for another...Let me please see my
Loving mother.*

*Doctor, doctor, please deliver me to my dad...So
That he too can be glad.*

*To both mom and dad, I'm new...Perhaps for dad,
You might have to show him what to do.*

*For your deeds a good wage you will earn...
For me, my name will be the first to learn.*

I'm Coming, Ready or Not

Hello, hello is this the hospital? I feel some
Labor pains... They come now and again.

Oh my goodness, I don't know what to
Do...Having a baby is an experience for me
That's new. Shall I boil some water?...I don't
Know if I'll have a son or daughter.

Hello hospital, I need some assistance...I feel
I'm losing resistance...I feel my body getting
Weak...Oh no, my water bag has just sprung
A leak.

I need some instructions and I need them
Now...With the pain I'm feeling, I need to lie
Down. Ooh, the pain is getting closer and
Stronger...I just can't wait any longer.

No one ever told me what this was all
About...Ooh, hello hospital, my child has just
Come out. My baby is a girl... She's the most
Beautiful in the world. Thank you for
Answering the telephone...And not leaving me
All alone. Please send the ambulance to get
me...So That they can see *my beautiful baby*.

The Blessed Baby

Oh beautiful, my baby child, your hazel eyes
Are now gray. Your purpose is for
Humanity...How beautiful is your name.

My baby child, my baby child, God blessed
Your dad and me. He said He would...I knew
He could. He'll bless you, dad, and me.

Baby's Arrival

I'm here now, for me it's a new town. Dear
Dad and mom help me to understand where I
Came from.

Soon we'll be going home...Now you and
Mommy are not alone. While taking me
Home, please do so gently...Just imagine, you
Had only me and not three.

When I get home, I'll want to eat...But you
Must first remove my size zero shoes from my
Tiny feet.

With my stretched out arms, I thank God
Above...For what's in store for me, your and
Mommy's precious love.

Milk Is A Natural

Dear Mommy,

Feed me with the milk from your breast...Many
Doctors, nurses and midwives say it's the
Best.

They also say that glass bottles cannot
Compare...Since I'm the baby around here,
There's no one else with whom to share.

The milk from your breast, I won't need for too
Long...I know that from this nutrition, I'll be big
And strong.

The nourishment I know...Will help me to grow
To love and appreciate the sun, rain and
Snow... what's more, I will make you proud of
Me wherever you go.

Changing Times

*Please, please will someone change my
Pamper or my diaper?...I'll then show you
I can get real hyper.*

*With smiles and laughter I'll jump up and
Down...When my odor is gone so will your
Frown.*

*Your face will be adorned with a smile...
Only until I present you with another pile.*

*Please, please change my pamper...And
Don't forget to put my dirty clothes in the
Hamper.*

Teach Me

Now teach me to walk...You've taught me to talk.
You can teach me how to eat...I already know how to sleep.

Teach me how to run...So we can continue to have lots of fun.

Teach me about the raven and the dove...
Most importantly, I need to be shown lots of love.

Baby Speaks to Daddy

Daddy, daddy, please respect my mommy...
Please show her the real loving man you can
be.

Hold her tightly in your arms...Let her see that
you really mean no harm.

Offer her a sweet lyric from a song...Let her
know that your treatment of her in the
past...That you were dead wrong!

Baby, Baby, Baby

Mommy, while I was not yet born from a car or
Truck I heard a horn. It frightened me so...
Inside you I was trapped, with no where to go.

From time to time I heard your sweet words
While you sat on the park bench, I heard the song
Birds. They sang their harmonious tune...Perhaps
It was during the month of June.

Mommy, I heard daddy claim you as his number
One lady...He would even call you baby. You
Made him feel special when you called him baby...
Although he was a big and strong man from the
Navy.

Now that I'm here, please let me be your only
Baby. So please just refer to daddy as your main
Man from the navy...And ask him to keep calling
You his number one lady.

The New Addition
We call...Semaj Jamahl

Mommy and daddy, please introduce me to
My sister and brother. Please explain to them
That they now have a new baby brother.

Please take time to teach them my name...I'm
Sure they'll be glad to have someone else to
Blame. Yes, blame... Blame for the behaviors
That would bring them shame.

Please explain to them that you must share
With me your unselfish love...Let them know
That for additional love, they can look to God
Above.

Please inform them that I can be not only a
Brother but a friend...And that I'll need a hug
Or a kiss every now and then.

The Miracle of Life

The date was February first, nineteen ninety five...If never
Before, we knew the baby was alive. It was about six
O'clock in the *morn*...This baby was ready to be *born*.

The labor pains were about ten minutes apart...To seek
Advice from the midwife would be smart. She said to
Hurry and come on in...registration and examination will
Begin.

Checked in and still dealing with the pain...moments later
The doctor and midwife came. In about two hours the
Birth was complete. I looked at the clock and it was
Twelve o'three.

The doctor said here is your joy...You have a beautiful
Baby boy! I was allowed to cut the umbilical cord...A
Couple of minutes later, another nurse walked through the
Door.

I told her 'His name is Semaj Jamahl'...His audible cry I
Know could be heard down the hall. Six pounds and
Twelve ounces was his weight...I held him with a *warm*
Embrace.

To him some soft songs I began to sing...I looked him in
The face, I know that one day he'll be a king. I looked to
My wife and said with a smile...'Thank you for another
Beautiful child.' The nurse clutched in her *arms* an
Informational note pad...I quickly stated that I am this
Baby's proud dad!

Why Weight?

What is so magical about the pounds people weigh? Our
society has unofficially endowed each of us with the
subliminal authority on health as it relates to weight.
We somehow use weight to sometimes establish the
character or determine the assessed value of a person.
At the announcement of a *newborn* baby most times the
very first question asked is: `Oh, how much does the baby
weigh?' This inquiry often supersedes the other pertinent
questions such as, `Is the baby healthy?' `What is the
baby's name?' or even if the mother is healthy?
For some lottery enthusiast, they are perhaps interested
in the weight of the baby for the use of the numbers.
Some feel that the weight of the newborn displayed in
numbers, offers a good winning chance.

Every *newborn* baby has the innate potential to be a
"winner" for itself, its community and our world. This
potential does not stem from any magical number
interpreted from a birth weight. It does in fact come from
its innocence and its ability to *learn* to respect him or
herself and others. This potential extends itself to this
child to be likewise respected. The character or the value
of a person could not or should not be measured by a
birth weight. The character should in fact be measured
by the positive contributions one makes towards
establishing a better society and world.At the
announcement of a *newborn* baby, the first question
should be `How can this child be nurtured to be all that it
can be?' This is most important if we are to plan for a
better society!

COMMUNITY AWARENESS

Musicians...Let's Band Together

I have some requests and some pleas to all musicians
And want-to-bees...It's time to wake up our community,
We need some real *unity*! Let's *form* an orchestra and a
Band, we need to unite and take a stand. For those who
Sing with a voice...Let this effort be your choice.

So lift your voice real loud, let's let them know we are
About to make some changes...So we need those who
Can sing in all ranges. To the passing cars, join in with a
Horn beep...Let's wake up those who are still asleep!
To those who play piano you must be bold and let your
Actions show. To those who play the organ so well... You
Must stop those *from* treating our community like hell.

To those who beat the drum, you must be on guard that
Our community is not viewed as a slum...To those who
Play the symbol, you must make our elected officials
Accountable. To the director who must direct, make sure
Our community doesn't suffer from abandonment and
Neglect. To those Who use the snare too, you must say
To those who destroy our youth... How dare you!
To those who play the saxophone, when you see crime
Occurring, you must dial 911 on the telephone. To those
Who play the violins, you can't afford to stand by in
Silence. There is a part for those who blow the *horn*
Help to keep our neighborhood from being *torn*. Another
Job for the director who must direct...Make sure all the
Musicians do their jobs, and that they and our community
Stay in check!

Respect or We'll Reject

We want to respect you in our
Community...Your leadership should bring
About unity.

You could very well be our example...Your
Respectful presence should be ample.

Your behavior should never cause
Disgrace...Your integrity we'll embrace.

Show us that you care...We know that your
Important decisions will be fair.

Stand *firm* for the issues that affect us...In our
Community we really need someone we can
Trust!

Invest In Us

WANTED: *All* Black Educated Professionals
Please return to the black
communities that you seem to
have forgotten about...
***

The *families* need your guidance.
The *elderly* need your comfort.
The *children* need your wisdom.
The *neighborhood children* need to see your
leadership.
The *community churches* need your spirit.
The *public schools* need your intellect.
The *neighborhood* need your taxes.
The *businesses* need your patronage.

Think about it...
You are that valuable to the entire
Community...There is no place like *home*!

No...Not Roxbury

Roxbury is a beautiful neighborhood...The
Media looks for the bad and ignores the good.

Sure, Roxbury has its problems, as does other
Towns...But nine out of ten stories reported,
Are orchestrated to produce frowns!

Now come on media, let's report the
Truth...And stop tearing down our youth.

When you tell the truth, your papers will still
Sell. Just stop treating Roxbury like a living
Hell!

Talk about its inner beauty. In time you will
Understand and the whole world will see!

If I Can Help Someone...Will I?

Poor, unemployed and disabled Jack and
Jill...Went to the State House on Beacon Hill,
To apply for food stamps. The legislators said
"No", below poverty level you must show.

They said, In fact the whole system will be
Revamped. So Jack and Jill went for help at
City Hall. The bureaucrats said "We're sorry,
We can't help you at all."

So Jill wrote a letter to the White House.
They said, "We're sorry but You have a
Spouse." So in poverty Jack and Jill will
Remain, forced to live on the streets in
Shame.

They were confused because they didn't
Understand the political game. The Federal,
State nor City Governments wanted to take
The Blame. Poor Jack and Jill later died from
Malnutrition...And the fifth *term* politician is on
The same streets trying to get signatures for
His Reelection petition. So let's remember
Poor Jack and Jill...And Don't forget that
Politician who's whacked and socially ill!

The Welfare Bureaucrat

The welfare system is the topic of the day.
Although for many years, the *whole system* has
been in disarray.

There is a misnomer that must be
rejected...Let the record of *truth* be reflected.

It's *not true* that most on welfare are
black...Most are white and that's a fact!

The system was created to keep people
down...It helped to create more ghettos...While
the more affluent steadily moved out of town.

Most of the money *doesn't* benefit those in
need...The money is mismanaged by
bureaucratic greed!

People should earn a living and not be given
something on a silver platter...At the same
time they should be given *equal* opportunity to
Climb the economic ladder. Help to educate
them. Many techniques and skills they'll
learn...With proper support, guidance and
opportunity, the money they need, they'll *earn*!

Family Dignity

There was a young lady who lived in a
Housing project...Just because she lived
There, everyone treated her with disrespect.

She was poor, her children numbered four.
The youngest was in Head start...But boy,
Was he smart!

When the bill collector called on the
Telephone, the kid would politely say, "My
Mommy is not home!"

The oldest child was eight...She said
"Mommy, don't worry, our situation will get
Better, just wait."

I will make you proud and happy. I will be a
Credit to society. I will show them that this
Family might be poor in wealth...But we will
Always be rich in spirit and in health.

No one will be able to again disrespect our
Family...Why? Because we have dignity!

A Letter to Mr. Rich Man

Dear Rich Man,

Where do you get off thinking that you are
Better than me... Just because you have
Millions of dollars and I have only a penny?

While your nerves are whacked...My spiritual
Soul is intact. You are a real snob...You feel
I'm not good enough for a job.

You'll throw food away...When I don't even
Have a place to stay! In spite of my situation,
Lifted high I keep my head...You don't care as
Long as you have a nice comfortable bed.

You sit there and think my situation is funny...
You really don't care, as long as you keep
Making money. Mr. Rich man, in your glory,
You are filled with smiles...But I say to you
"Just wait awhile." I will not always be poor. I
Just need the *opportunity* and no more!

Don't forsake others because tables do
Turn...All it takes is one match and all your
Material wealth could burn!

What's Your Price?

The American system of rewards is crazy. It's
More than crazy, it's sick...A guy can be paid
Millions for swinging a hockey stick. It gives
Roses to those who should receive daisies.
For example, sports figures are paid millions
Of dollars...They do *substantially* less work
Than the blue collars.

It's often the blue collars who risk their health,
But it's the sports figures who reaps the
Wealth! High pay should be given to teachers
Of *education*...But no, high pay goes to the
Baseball players on spring vacation.

Relatively small money is paid to this person
Who fight fires...But no, ten times as much is
Paid to an umpire! A crafts person will earn
$200. to build a casket...while a basketball
Player will earn $1000. even if he misses a
Basket. Look at the people in child care.
They make pennies compared to those ball
Players who are paid millions, for the uniforms
They wear...Look at this country and all the
Wealth it could share, if only all our systems
Of justice would care and be a lot more fair!

Truth or Consequences

America, America, if you continue to feed us
With your lies about the cleanliness of the CIA
And the FBI...

Those who don't know different will keep
Accepting your stories as truth...But one day it
Will be exposed like a rotten tooth!

The fabricated stories will grow and mount like
A tidal wave...They will eventually ignite and
Explode like a hand grenade!

It will burn and perhaps disfigure law
Enforcement officers and their political
Ties...The whole world will know that for years
And years, it has been sold a pack of lies!

Please let the truth be known...Our children
From the sixties are now grown. Please tell
Us the truth...It's important for our youth.

The youth of today are not so patient and
Kind...The lies they were told, really messed
Up their minds. No more lies, no more, no
More. God knows we don't need another civil
War!

Military Veterans

America, you must take care of your Military
Vets. Remember, they risked their lives in
Those fighter bomber jets! Some really
Sacrificed their health...Just so You can
Maintain your material wealth.

They went so far as to promise to fight...even
Though their mission may not always be
Politically right. Some went in on a volunteer
Basis, they agreed to defend all races.

We know that some risked their lives for land
Or oil the bottom line is otherwise some major
Business deals would spoil. You contend that
It was to save this country...So that every
Man, woman and child Would be free.

Let's stop treating our Veterans like a freak...If
It were not for them, our beautiful language
We would probably not be allowed to speak.

Veterans are important, whether or not they
Got hit with a military shell...They all need to
Be taken care of *very well*!

The Shame Game

America, you should be ashamed of
yourself...You will do anything for your
material wealth. You have inducted
generations of women and mostly men on
which you played a dirty game. Shame,
shame, shame...You told them they could be
all they wanted to be...but instead you stuck
them out in the jungles and on the raging
seas! You went into your smoke-filled office
and closed the door...but because you would
be protected, you declared war.

You tried to explain the reason, but you lied...
You know what happened? Many innocent
Americans died. Those who made it back
showed their faces only to receive another
slap. You are quick to honor the *dead*...But
many of the living Vets don't even have a
decent bed.

You spent millions on a marble wall...At the
VA hospitals the administration dread the
phone calls. Remember, these Veterans have
families to support...But all you're worried
about is how *patriotic* you look on your annual
report!

Drug Control Patrol

Let's reveal the real beneficiaries of illegal
Drugs...The "Man" infiltrates our
Neighborhoods, and then call our young men,
"Thugs."

The drug transaction is all about power and
The almighty dollar...The "Man" is no where
Around when the addict screams and hollers.

The distribution of marijuana, heroin or
Crack...Will cause the young fifteen year old
To get shot in his Back.

The possession of these drugs will offer the
Illusion of power...It's so powerful it will make
The dealer and the user stay Up for twenty
Four hours.

The "Man" should really be ashamed...In fact,
For a change, the "Man" should experience
The pain.

A Rap with a Police Officer

Hey, Police Officer,

I'm a big shot twelve year old with a nine
millimeter...Don't worry about me, go after the
wife beater. He'll get more time than me...In
fact, prison, you'll be lucky if I ever see!

Sure, arrest me if you choose...This case
you'll sure to lose. This system doesn't know
what to do with kids my age...I'll be back on
the streets next time with a twelve gauge!

No one ever made me set a priority...So I'll do
what I want and then blame it on society! The
courts won't allow my parents to discipline...I
never went to church to know if my behavior
was a sin. In my twelve years, I've been
placed in seven different schools...Huh, I'm so
cool, I get to make my own set of rules.

Pretend you don't see me, I insist...Or I'll put
you on my hit list. As I said, see me and turn
your head...Because if you look at me too
hard, I just might shoot you dead!

The Gang Organization

Not-so-wise Ronald belonged to a gang...The
Gang was so organized, it had it's own slang.
Each member is required to own a
Beeper...More clout is earned, as into the
Gang they get deeper. All members are
Ordered to carry a gun...Some could be found
With more than one. The normal wear is a
Black hooded jacket and big military-style
Boots...By the way, in terms of the guns they
Carry...Most of them don't even know how to
Shoot.

They claim that their membership for them
Establishes identity...They don't realize that in
The gang they won't find serenity. The gang's
Main interests are drugs, guns, and so-called
Respect...For these they, without problem, will
Break someone's Neck. Oh, another real
Issue for them is turf...If they had their way,
They would take over the whole earth! Poor
Ronald really doesn't realize what he's
Into...His gang will make him later regret the
Things he'll now do. Right now Ronald must
Feel he's cool...But the reality is, he's a fool.
This is a bad path to tread...Ronald, get out
Before you be found dead!

Crack on Jack

Poor gullible Jack...Was convinced by his so-
Called friends, to try some crack.

They told him to take just one hit...Only a little
High, that's all you'll get. Just one hit of
Crack, that's all it took...To capture and control
Jack on his way to being *hooked*!

Crack for Jack was soon A big demand...He
Stole and then sold everything on which he
Put his hands. He was later arrested in
Several drug raids...In a short time he got ill
And was diagnosed with AIDS.

Jack looked to his friends...So-called. They
Said "We're sorry, we can't help you at all."
What happened to you is a shame...But don't
Look to us, we're not to blame. You should
Have known that crack is a killer of its own
Kind...You should not have been so
Weak...You should have used your own mind.

Jack had a moment to reflect on his partying,
Being cool and all his thefts...He didn't realize
That he would allow others to lead him to his
Slow and painful Death!

All Are Created but Not Treated Equal

Judge me for who I am...To be inferior
Because I'm black is a scam. Sit down and
Feel free to ask me questions...I'll assess your
Inquiries and then make some suggestions.

I'll recommend that you really open your
Mind...An educated and well informed person
You'll find. I'm not that worthless person you
Think I might be...In fact, my ancestors and I
Helped to build this country.

We're *not* asking for something for free...We
Simply deserve an equal opportunity. We
Have exerted blood, sweat, an tears...But
What remains a shame is after all these, we
Still remain in fear. We know that bigots and
Racists will judge us for the color of our
Skin...Nature should declare racism to be *the*
Sin of all sins.

We are denied access to fair housing,
Education and work...By some selfish,
Ignorant racist jerks. So let's be judged by
Our character content...And we'll realize that
Our external appearance is irrelevant.

Bids or Bull?

In terms of business, that minority "set aside" stuff is a
Joke...I'm wise to the game. They think I just awoke! I
Think the plan is designed to isolate...So they can
Systematically discriminate. You see, they put us in a
Separate book...So that when they need to cover their
Butts, they know just where to look! The buyers already
Have their favorite suppliers selected...But I know from
Experiences...Those who get rejected. Sometimes the
Calls are placed at the very last minute asking for a bid. I
Say to myself, "Okay, who are they trying to kid?" Other
Times they'll request all kinds of information...I know it's
So they can use it in their process of elimination.

More than likely the decision was already made...The
Paperwork was probably being processed for the vendor
To get paid. You see, the premise is that they don't want
You to make a dime...So they don't have to worry about
You the next time. Then when they're called-on for their
Action...They can say `look, we have met our fraction.'
Either the minority firms are too small, too high or too
Late...I don't know why they don't choose to participate.

These private and government institutions need to be
Accountable...Their institutional discriminatory practices,
The whole world should know. Then maybe these entities
Won't look so nice...So that next time they think about that
"Set aside stuff", maybe they'll think twice. I'm sure there
Are some sincere buyers...But then the rest are liars. To
Those who don't think this is true...Set up your business
And watch it happen to you!

Tunnel Vision

Mr. Merchant, where is your respect for Me?...Treat me
With some dignity. Don't you know that you shouldn't bite
The hand that feeds you...What I'm about to tell you is the
Truth.

You show your subtle racism in many ways...It has
Happened for many years and months, in fact, everyday.
Every time I come to your store to purchase your
Hardware...The minute I walk in the door, you greet me
With a stare.

Before I can say "How do you do", you yell out "Can I
Help you?" You act like I'm going to steal something... So
You seem to be annoyed when the telephone rings. You
Don't know if you should get the phone in a hurry...Or if
You should keep your eyes on me and worry. You
Summon other clerks to watch my every action...But when
I approach the check out counter you begin smiling for
The money you'll make in this transaction.

I'll place the money in your hand but on the counter you
Put my change down with a slam! I have every right in
The world to complain but you have the nerve to tell me
To please "Come again."

I later thought that his treatment of me was abrupt. I
Figured, well, if enough of us resist, one day perhaps,
He'll be bankrupt.

Oh, by the way Mr. Merchant, while you are so busy
Watching "My kind",...guess what? Your own people are
Robbing you blind!

Oh...What a Night

At midnight, I sit quietly in my living room...All
Of a sudden, I hear a violent sound that went
Boom!

I rushed to the window but all I saw was the
Peacefully quiet falling snow! I heard a
Distant car horn...But all I saw was my
neighbor's Lights go on!

Minutes of silence went by...I figured it was
Time for me to sigh!

Just then I heard the siren of a police
Vehicle...But from my window, all I could see
Were growing ice cycles!

The next day I inquired as to the siren I heard
Last night...I was told that a man was reported
To be homeless and suffered with frost bite!

What was that noise that went boom?...Out of
A trash filled can, came a vicious Raccoon!

I'm glad this doesn't happen everyday of the
Week...Or else I would never get to sleep!

Don't Judge the Book By Its Cover

These poems are offered by me, the writer...I can't
Help it but I'm a fighter.

For my first book, I was concerned about my
Photo on the cover...I didn't want my book to be
Prejudged because of my skin color. I felt that
The content was important, so back to the printer
I Went. Lucy, I said "scratch the photo idea...My
Skin color will generate tremendous Fear.

My book, some whites will not embrace because
Of my black face! The education and information
In the book, I wanted to Be accepted. But my
Black face on the cover would perhaps make the
Book rejected.

Now I understand, that is their problem for which
They must deal. I'm going to proudly show my
Face and say what I feel.

Perhaps these poems will make you smile or cry
When you start. But what I say and how I say it
Comes right from the heart. Well, seek the
Meaning, I employ these poems I hope you will
Enjoy!

A Letter to My Wife

Dear Maritza,

Thank you for sticking with me through thick
And thin... You've helped me in so many
Ways, to count them, I don't know where I
Would begin.

You've supported all my new ideas...You sat
Attentive and showed me you Care.

No one else could compare to you...No one
Else could support me the way you do.

You've given me love, support and
Understanding from the start for all that, I love
You from the bottom of my heart.

The Love Question

Dear Maritza,

This is the night that *I ask for your hand in marriage,* so that one day we together can push the same baby carriage.

...Will you marry me?

A Son's Love

I dearly love my mother...The sacrifices she
Made could not be made by a sister or a
Brother.

For nine months she carried me...I could not
Repay her with words or a fee.

A precious love cannot be bought...To me,
Love, honor and respect she taught. In all my
Endeavors she stood beside...Most times it
Was only she in whom I could confide.

I'm happy to say that I never brought my
Mother to shame if I were to misbehave, she
Would not be the one to blame.

She taught me that if I loved and respected
My mother, I could love and respect my
Wife...To have and to hold for life.

She is not only my mother, but she's my
Mom...She told me to never forget where I
Came from! She taught me things without
Really knowing...With the continued proper
Direction, I know where I'm going!

A Letter to My Mother

Dear Mother,

Thank you for the way you raised me...The tough times you had to endure, it's a wonder you're not crazy.

Growing up on welfare wasn't easy...I cried when the school kids teased me. I'm sorry for being so wild...I should have realized that I was not your only child. You made sure I went to school...You taught me that education was my most valuable tool.

Now that I'm a grown man...In retrospect, your teachings I understand. You encouraged me to be the best...It didn't matter if I wore a T-shirt or a tie and vest. You had a big smile at my graduation Processional...For you knew that I would be an outstanding legal professional. As a lawyer I expect to win my case...mom, I wish to say something to you Face to face.

As a lawyer, my character will be judged by my merit...To you mom, I give God and you the credit.

Dear Mommy

Dear Mommy,

There are a few things I'd like to tell. First of all, I want to thank you for the sacrifices you've made to have me. Next, I want to say that I am blessed to be as healthy as I am in spite of all the junk foods and illegal substances you fed to me when I was encapsulated in your womb.

For nine months I was helpless, I could not really convey to you that I didn't appreciate what you were giving me. On occasion, I found the strength to cause you to regurgitate some of those substances that were too intolerable for me. I had to deal with tobacco, alcohol, and the steady flow of sugar residue, from all those sweets you consumed.

For my sake, you could have laid off of all those salty and spicy foods. Ha, you thought you felt the burning in your chest, I felt it all over. Mommy, please take better care of yourself, so that you can live a long healthy life for you and me. Thank you Mommy.

Father

My Father who stands five feet seven...for me,
Dad will be your name. Yes, problems will
come...Many sacrifices will be done, from birth
even past the age of eleven.

At this time I say, be proud and lift your head
and be sure to watch your steps, things will
only get better. One day you'll get caught,
engaged in meditation

You'll pray that I'll keep from evil. That I'll be
smart and not dumb. At any hour, you'll hear
a story whenever and wherever again.

The Lord's Prayer (excerpt from St. Matthew 6: 9-13)

Our Father which art in heaven,
Hallowed by Thy name.
Thy kingdom come.
Thy will be done
In earth as it is in heaven.
Give us this day our daily bread.
And forgive us our debts,
 as we forgive our debtors
And lead us not into temptation,
But deliver us from evil.
For Thine is the kingdom and the power
 and the glory forever. Amen.

Dear Big Brother

Dear Big Brother,

I'm glad we share the same father and
Mother. I've never told you about my true
Feelings...But there is a struggle with which
I'm having difficulty dealing.

I know I have to be me, and that I'm trying to
Do...But what I'd rather be is just like you!

You seem to be perfect at whatever you
Undertake...Not even one error I saw you
Make.

Please talk to me and let me know that I am
Okay for who I am. Otherwise, continue to be
My idol, I'll follow your lead...When I become
Great like you, you'll know that in me, you
Have planted a seed.

Teach me to set priority...so that I will be a
Real credit to society...

Our parents we'll make glad...Big brother,
Between you and me, you could be my
Second dad!

A Letter to Ruthie

Dear Ruthie,

You are so special to me, I enjoy our
Conversations...You are filled with information.

I enjoy our talks about the blessings of God...I
Appreciate your encouragement, especially
When you give me the nod.

When I have an idea that I think is nice
Sometimes you will say, "Wait a minute, would
You run that by me twice."

When I seek a second opinion, I ask for your
Advice. You sometimes tell me that A little
More thought might suffice.

Up until now you have not lead me wrong.
You tell me to pray on it and I'll get good
Results before long.

Kysha's Cookies
"Why Settle For Crumbs"

I have a niece named Kysha...Interested in
Business she wants me to teach her. She
Says I'm her role model indeed...Practical and
Technical business Information she really
Needs.

So I helped her get started with her own
"gig"...I let her know that her business must
Be small before it can be big! Homemade
Cookies are what she makes...I tell her that to
Have a good business, good products, good
Service and good prices are what it takes.

Also, I tell her that her homemade cookies will
Really sell if they have a unique taste, touch,
And smell! What's most important is to pay
Close attention to your clients...Because they
Have the power to stagnate your business
Growth or make you a giant!

Tough times may come and provoke some
Tears...But hang in there and move forward
And you'll be in business for many years!

Thank God for Johnson Enterprises

To Sandra of Johnson Enterprises...How do
You stay so energized? You seem to work
Around the clock...Your office door is *never*
Locked*!* You never run out of supplies I
See...A professional businesswoman with
Expertise. You have *earned **two*** Master
Degrees...What a feat*!* ...Your clients agree.

When I call you, you never seem to be short
Of time... When others might say, "My
Time...Your dime." Your business represents
The `State of the Art'...Being able to offer the
Best, is a move that is smart*!* Your services
Are set at a *more than* reasonable price...For
Those on a budget, you don't have to think
Twice. Regardless of the amount of work,
Whether small or vast...Sandra, you sure do
Work fast*!*

There are very good qualities about your
Business that are real nice...*Excellent* services,
Products, cost, and most important, it's
Precise. Your business is not another "Fly by
Night"...It's the place to go when you need
Something done right*!*

Thank You Teacher

Dear Ms. Brown,

I traveled from the other side of town. I came
To visit you at the Dearborn Middle School...I
Came to testify of your unique teaching Rules.

Your were my teacher in grade six...Your
Diverse knowledge in basic subjects gave me
A fine educational mix. You have helped me
To know myself...You have taught me that it's
Okay to have plenty of books on the shelf.

In all of your students, you've shown great
Concern...Although some seemed to not want
To learn.

This visit to you is simply to say "thanks"...I
Personally feel I've moved up the ranks. I see
Some former classmates going to the bar...I
Want you to know that I'm your shining star.

Ms. Brown, those good o'le days I
Miss...Again, I want to thank you with a hug
And a kiss.

Teach My Child

Dear Teacher,

I am writing this letter with great concern...because I am sending my son to school to learn. I want him to learn the latest theories of math...Please teach him about the important historical path.

Teach him the *truth* about Black History...Show him that Black History is no mystery!

He'll need to know how to read...Instill in him that his true history is his foundational seed!

Teach him laboratory and behavioral science...So as an adult, he'll know what it is to be self reliant. Make sure he learns to write...So that he, through words, can win any literary fight.

Please prepare him for college...Let him know that in life real power is achieved through *knowledge*!

Stop Calling Me Boy!

For progress sake, stop calling me "*Boy*"...I am not a boy!

I'm a married man....Boys don't have wives!

I'm the father of three...Boys don't have babies!

I've earned my Master's Degree...Boys don't go to graduate school!

I'm a business owner...Boys don't own businesses!

I'm a homeowner...Boys don't buy houses!

You need to elevate me to the next level...Call me a *man*!

Those "Boy" days for black men are over and long gone...Treat me with respect!

Empower me with dignity...I will then appreciate *your* mere *existence*!

AIDS
Act If Death Scares

To all males, especially black males, I want to
Discuss an issue that is serious...It's about a
Virus that is deadly and mysterious.

AIDS is the name of this killer...You can bet
Your life it's not a thriller! It has taken away
The common man, as well as the stars... It
Doesn't really care who you are!

I speak to the black male because in number
We are being reduced...By sex and drugs, we
Are being seduced. In many ways our
Numbers are being diminished...Some won't
Be satisfied until We're finished.

With the AIDS, knives, guns, drugs, and
Alcohol we drink...If we don't be careful, we
Will soon be *extinct*!

So let's be careful who our partners are...If not
We could receive a deadly scar. And let's
Change our behavior...And look to Jesus as
Our savior!

Harmonizing Stars

To the Harmonizing Stars, assemble
Yourselves to render an "A" or "B"
Selection...The first one should offer direction.

Your audience should be encouraged to join
In...and blend their voices as soon as you
Begin.

Make sure you sing every verse of the
Song...But just don't sing it *too* long.

Now for the selection "B"...Sing it slow and
Sweet.

Make sure you leave a thought with the
Crowd... Remember it should not be
Performed too loud.

It should be done soft and sweet...With the
Perfect blend of harmonies, your listening
Audience will be blessed with a treat!

Advice From a Stranger

Thank you sir for your advice...I'm so glad I
Thought twice.

You told me to put the stick down...Your
Advice was meaningfully sound.

I don't know what made me want to do
Wrong...I now realize that my self respect is
Not that strong.

My self-esteem I know I must build...Because
In my heart is disrespect and malice filled.

In my life I need more encouragement and
Correction...With that I know I'll be headed in
The right direction.

I need to be respectful and loving of others
More often...Before I end up in my own coffin!

FRIENDSHIP

Here and Now

Now that I'm here, you can wipe away your
Tears. Just hold me tightly in your arms...I
Will be at ease with your charm.

Promise me that I will always be your baby...
Whatever you do, please don't say maybe.

I need the assurance, particularly at this
Time...Say with a big voice to my little ears,
That you will always be mine.

Friends For Keeps

*Go away rain, Go away rain...The constant
Pounding reminds me of the pain. Yes, the
Pain of being without you...I feel mentally
Trapped, not knowing where to go or what
To do.*

*Please come sun. Please come sun. The
Constant rays remind me of the good o'le
Days. Yes, the good o'le days, we had fun
In all kinds of ways. We traveled around
The world we talked and played like a
Little boy and girl.*

*We sometimes argued, but we were sure to
Make up. Because God knows we didn't
Want to break up. I don't like the thought
Of being sad...The thought of you and
Being with you is what always makes me
Glad.*

I Need You

Oh, how I need you. I get joy when I'm able
To please you...I get thrills when I tease
And squeeze you.

Please come back for awhile...I miss your
Touch and your smile.

Let's Stay Together

Let's make our friendship last...Let's not
Dwell on the past. It is time to let a new
Love be born...Looking to the future, let's
Move on.

Let's try a new trend...Whatever we do,
Don't let our friendship end.

I guess I'm saying the same thing in more
Than one way...The point is, let's start us A
New thing today.

A Message to My Beautiful Black Man

Listen to me my beautiful black man...This is
Your beautiful black woman speaking to you
Again.

Our relationship needs to be much stronger...
I just can't deal with your *games* much longer.

I respect all of your credentials...But you are
Not living up to your fullest potential.

You need to get your act together...And stop
Changing moods like the Weather.

I know you're under a lot of pressure...I don't
Need to feel any lesser.

Show me your love *all* the time...I don't want to
Keep guessing if you're only mine.

I realize that you are a workaholic...But when
You're gone so long, I get nostalgic.

Spend more time with me...I'll be the lock
And you can be the key.

I want you to enter my mind and heart
And we shall never again be apart!

GENERAL

Money

Money is an interesting instrument...The
Bottom line is that it's designed to be spent.

It's amazing what some people will buy...
It sometimes determines if you will live or die!

It can produce fortune or fame...It can really
Bring out shame.

Some people let money go to their head...
Considerable inheritances will make some
Forget about the dead.

Some people will sure change their attitudes...
It will make the naturally meek turn rude.

For money, some parents will even sell their
Children...It will cause some people to forsake
Their friends.

Money can keep you from being out in the
Cold...But it can *never, ever* save your soul!

To No Return

I was kidnapped from foreign soil thousands of miles away. I was given sunlight and fed water, my growth was monitored. My quality was classified. When I was good enough and mature enough, I was sold for next to nothing in my own country.

I was packed up and sent on a one-way trip to the United States of America. I arrived in Florida, only to be met by some uniformed custom agents, who had the nerve to inspect and judge my characteristics to see if I was "good enough" to enter the USA.

...So I was. They felt I was "good enough", so I was assessed another fee. From there I was again sold for another dollar amount... Because there were so many of us raised together, we were sold for a discount at auction.

I then took flight to Boston, where I would be sold again. I am now purchased by a florist, who will give me water and then fashion me and bring out the beauty in me.

Later, I will be transported to a host family and be allowed to rest comfortably on the mantle for all eyes to see. I'll remain there until I die.

The Motherland

This is a king talking to his Nubian queen...
Our beautiful motherland--Have you seen?

It is still enriched with precious gold...
There are some resources that haven't yet been sold.

We still have the richness of our culture and
Traditions...Much of our visual beauty is on worldwide
Exhibitions.

We should return to the land from where we've come...
We could be entertained by the sounds of the native
Drum.

We could feast on our cultural menus...We could
Assemble amongst the natives for a traditional dance
Without these European shoes!

Our spirits could be blessed with the ceremonial fire...
We could even wear African attire.

So, I say to you my queen, get the travel agent on the
Telephone...Guess what! We are going back home...

Please come, may I have your hand...Let's go *back*
To the *Motherland!*

History Teacher

Teacher, teacher, how could you survive your
Job so long...For twenty years you taught
History *so wrong!*

You taught that in 1492...Columbus discovered
The ocean blue.

You taught that he discovered the USA!...Did
You know that the Native American Indian was
Here *many years* before that day?

Before you continue to teach...Perhaps into the
Trenches of history you should reach.

Some facts might seem kind of hazy...But
When you see the truth, you'll admit that what
You've taught for twenty years was absolutely
Crazy!

What You See...Is Not All You Get

You might see me as chunky or obese...But
My heart is lovingly sweet. I might be hefty
And not difficult to find...But I can be ever so
Kind.

You might look at me and say, "I think you're
Getting fatter."...But I say,"What you think
Doesn't matter." You might think that I am
Limited at what I can do...but you should know
That this shouldn't concern you!

Of course, you're thinking that I'm not
Healthy...but with my skills and will, I have the
Power to be financially wealthy!

You think that only food is what makes me
Thrive...No, I say, I love life, it's good to be
Alive! Most people think we're lazy...That
Thought, how stupid and crazy.

Your insensitive words and thoughts can
Sometimes leave a scar...But the best way to
Deal with us is to love and respect us for who
We are!

Don't Even Try It

At my physical challenge, please don't laugh...
But for grace you could be walking down the
Same path. I am not totally restricted...Many
Of my thoughts and abilities are unpredicted.

My physical abilities, you might have a
Doubt...But be careful, think about what
Physical ability you could do without!

You don't know what's in store for your future
To come...If you experienced what I have,
You'll know it's no fun.

It's my condition with which I must deal....
Treat me with respect and watch how much
Better I feel.

If you don't know what to say...I ask that if you
Know about prayer, please pray...I don't need
Your dollar or your dime...I just want your
Respect, and I'll be just fine!

The Football Game

At the sound of the whistle...Get ready to take
Off like a missile.

Charge for the one who has the ball...Just
Don't be afraid to fall.

Some guys will be small, Some will be tall...
You might be provoked to brawl, but you must
Listen for the referee's call.

Many people will be at this football
Game...Some players will one day make it to
The hall of fame.

Some spectators will watch the game for the
Thrill...The freezing temperature will inflict on
The guests, a bitter chill.

Some people will come and place their bet...If
It rains, everyone will get wet.

The object of the game is that it be won...The
Process should be all about having fun.

INSPIRATION

Be Yourself

Never be ashamed of who you are...Just
Remember, you are a shining star.

Don't try to be something you're not...Because
Somewhere down the road, you'll get caught.

For when your true identity is
Revealed...People will have known all the time
That you were not real.

You are like karats of fine gold. You might be
10, 14, 18 or more...You are precious no
Matter if you're rich or poor.

Your value should not be measured by your
Material wealth...You have all you need with a
Soul, clean heart and good health.

Don't Talk Trash

When you speak to me, select the words with substance. Choose the words in the context that will be allowed to enter my drums and then impede the inner faculties of my mind.

Make sure it has positive value, otherwise, I will compile and transmit it to the small and large intestine and prepare it for rapid disposal.

It will find its way to the reservoir of meaningless rhetoric!

Teach Me — I Want To Learn

Stop being so critical...You should be more
Spiritual.

If I need some assistance...Don't sit back and
Display your resistance.

If you know something that I don't...Show me,
And don't say you won't.

I'm sure from your wisdom I could benefit...I'm
Here waiting for you to submit.

I want to learn...Please understand my
Concern.

Since I need help and you're so bright...
Teach me the way, and I'll do what's right!

Youth...Our Future

Let's put our youth to work, then we won't be
So quick to call them jerks! In them we could
Put our confidence... Otherwise, we might be
A hindrance. Let's give them a growing
Chance... their present skills, we can help to
Enhance. Some methodologies may need
Correction...We could then set the youth in the
Right direction.

Let's be patient and understanding...At the
Same time, let's keep high standards and be
Supportively demanding. As they begin to
Learn...Let us show great concern. Some will
Excel and want to explore...Let us not be
Afraid to show them even more. They all
Deserve our respect...regardless of their
Intellect. The success of our efforts won't be
Complete, until we get all our youth off the
Streets. Let's work with them and keep them
From being lost...You never know, they could
Grow and show promise and one day be your
Boss!

It's the merchants in this case who have the
Power...Even if the youth are employed for
Only one hour. If they're working, they can't
Be on the streets to rob...So as merchants,
Let's do our part and give them a job!

A Message To Young Girls

Babies having babies...This didn't just begin in the
eighties. This has been happening for years...It has
caused many families to shed tears. Parents would rather
first see their daughter as a wife...Rather than to create a
new and innocent life. At a young age many are only
interested in smiling at boys...They then feel they have no
use for their Christmas toys. Many young girls don't know
what to do...to properly raise a child, they have absolutely
no clue.

These new babies, to the parents and grandparents are
often tossed... Otherwise, in this crazy world they become
lost. Some feel that a baby is what they need...The real
shame is some don't even know how to read.

Without the proper skills and resources they look to
people with money or food to spare...If that's not
available, they will resort to welfare. The system will
provide enough to barely make it...It will tell you, if you
want it...you better take it!

Oftentimes the burden falls on the mother of the
child...While the daddy is out there acting wild.
While you are the one to stay up most of the night...You
and your child will alone, have to deal with your plight.
So young girls, these facts you can't say you've never
known...Just remember you have to raise this child most
oftentimes on your own. So think about your future and
what you want to do...Don't let this childhood-motherhood
happen to you! Think about loving yourself...And put that
planned parenthood book back on the shelf!

Stop, Look and Listen

Stop! Young man...Drop that stick right from
Your hand.

Don't hit that old lady and commit a crime...If
You do, you will be facing prison time!

Once behind bars your whole future will be
Marked...With emotional scars.

You'll be under someone else's control...You'll
Be lucky if you later get parole.

Stop! Young man...You must understand that
If you hit that old lady and she dies...You
Might be ordered the electric chair and
Sentenced to "fry."

So listen I tell you...what I'm saying is true.
Think about it, you're about to hit someone's
Mother or wife...and you'll sadly ruin your
Whole life!

Wrong Direction or Right-of-Way?

To the ten, eleven or twelve year old who carries a nine
Millimeter gun... I say to you, you are headed in a
Direction that is not fun. Don't let the power of that gun
Go to your head as I said...In the direction you're headed,
You'll be dead.

Come here, let me give you a big hug and tell you how
Special you are...You know you have the potential to be a
Superstar!

You have a possible long life ahead of you...So lend an
Ear, open your eyes and you'll see what I'm saying is
True.

You apparently have missed something from birth...You
Haven't been taught to appreciate your self worth.

You can be all that you want or ought...You just have to
Be properly taught. From the time you were a baby with
A bottle...You were not blessed with the right role models.

It's not completely too late...let's look forward and start
With a clean slate. Tell me what's on your mind...A whole
New outlook on life I guarantee you'll find.

First, you must learn to respect yourself...then respect
Others. Don't worry about the fact that you have no
Brothers. You can look to the Lord who will be your
guide...He will Always be by your side. I'll be there for
your inspiration ...It's very important for you and me,
because you are Indeed our future generation!

S Blank X

Who said that life doesn't begin at
Conception? Could it be just hot air or factual
Rejection?

Is it a subject feared by some intellectuals,
Who see the human anatomy as only sexual?

The words sex and sexual often have a
Connotation of "Tabu."...Let's face it, without
Sex or conception, there would not be a me or
A you.

So let's not be afraid to work to understand
The process of birth...Certainly the subject is
Meaningful to all living matter on earth.

Again, I say, let's study the subject and
Enhance our minds...A new appreciation and
Understanding we will be sure to find.

Discipline Disputed

I am so confused, someone said while I was a
Child I Was abused. But of course I don't
Remember, I couldn't say if it was in January
Or December.

I now need to know the truth about this
Alleged abuse was I molested?...I know I was
Never arrested. Oh, I get it! Psychologists
Now say...I've been abused if I were made to
Obey.

I remember back in the day...To respect
Authority was the only way. I'm so grateful
For my upbringing as a child...Without the
Discipline I would be so wild.

I would have been out of control...Who knows,
I might be six feet under and frozen cold. I
Am so happy for the way I was raised...This
Statement to some would make them amazed.

Some may even say that I'm odd...I say that's
Okay, because I trust in God. I know that if I
Treat others with respect and love...I will be
Blessed by God above!

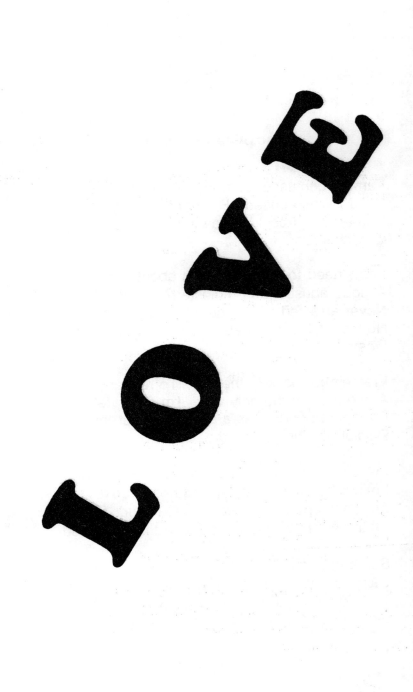

Let's Communicate

Tell me
Explain to me
Describe to me
Teach me
Share with me
Please whatever you do...
Show me love.

Affection

Kiss me with the lips on your lovely face
Face me at any time with the apple of
your eye
Eyeball me as I come into your hands
Hand me a note expressing
The greatest sentiments of your love
Love me with every beat of your heart!

Feelings

Talk to me, I have ears
Show me, I have eyes
Touch me, I have feelings
Explain to me, I have a mind
Love me, I have a heart!

The All Occasion Rose

I give these roses to you
For no special reason...
Because true love has its place
Any and every season.

I give these roses to you
For no special occasion...
But then again,
Every occasion is special with you.

The Powerful Rose

I am a beautiful rose...I can get a door open that has been closed.

Closed to the one that has done wrong...I can remain short or long.

I have a natural fragrance...I'm like a main ingredient to romance.

I have the appeal...To make soft a heart of steel.

My most popular color is red...My petals can be sprinkled all over a Bed.

To the sad, I can sooth the sorrow...I can bring joy for today and tomorrow.

For me only a few dollars you'll need to spend... Just me alone is the perfect thing to send.

I am that beautiful rose.

The Love I Feel

*I give these roses to you...I feel it's a nice thing
To do. I want to be with you like a hand in
Glove...I need to share with you my
unconditional Love.*

*Your body is what I want to caress...The thought
Of being without you would sure cause duress.*

*I need for my good thoughts to come true...Those
Thoughts are you loving me and me loving you!*

Angel of Love

May
Your
Birth
Angel
Bless
You

The Love Takeover

Love offers surprise...I want to be hypnotized.
Dig into the deeper canals of my mind...
Nothing but *thoughts of loving you*, you will find.

They say that cold hands means warm heart...
Hold me tightly and let the romance start.
Listen to my heartbeat...And let our spirits of
Love meet.

Sing to me a gentle song...Let's let the thrill
Of being together last long.

Please don't ever say good-bye...Just whisper
Softly to me good night.

Now I expect to see you the next day...To be
Reminded of the foreplay.

Yes, foreplay I say...That is what got us loving
Each other this way.

Oh, How Beautiful

Waking up in the morning
is as beautiful as
performing an honest days' work...
is as beautiful as
sitting down to a scrumptious hot meal...
is as beautiful as
lying in a comfortable bed...
is as beautiful as
dreaming of you...

Lonely Love

As I look out the window...I see a lonely dove
As a symbol...Of our departed love.

Now I'll close the shade...And think about the
Love we've made. I'll get on with my
Life...Although I wish you were my wife.

I think about our favorite song...The words
Say: "I don't see nothing wrong" with our
Break up...I see something wrong...The
Mystery is that I don't know for how long.

Marvin Gaye sang "There's nothing wrong with
Me loving you"...Let's take heed and make
That true. No matter what the weather...For
Love sake, let's get back together.

A Handle on Love

Search for me as you would your most perfect
China cup in your cupboard. When you find
me, hold me gently and securely as you would a
newborn baby. Place your lips tenderly on mine
as you would the piping hot brim of a tea cup.

Then look into my eyes, as you would look
through a pair of binoculars. Focus on my
pupils and read my thoughts, as you would read
a love story.

Watch my developing bright smile, as you would
watch the impeding sunrise above the distant
mountains. Whisper to me softly "I Love You",
as you would blow lightly to distinguish a small
butane from a birthday cake candle.

Who's To Blame?

Who's to blame for a new love that has just presented itself to me? This is the prevailing but unanswered question. Who's to blame for the new love that has just presented itself to me? Shall I be so naive and blame fate?...Or shall I shamefully blame the male Trait? Who's to blame for this new love that every male has just got to know her name? Maybe it's because they want to run their own game...In my book she's a real lady and not a dame! Who's to blame for her beauty so great? For how many generations back shall I Go?...Was it the genes of her great grands, grands, or parents...I'll never know. Who's to blame when many guys run to her like a reporter?...Close attention is paid to her, as though she's a favorite song often heard on a tape recorder.

Maybe it's her smile...Maybe it's her style
Maybe it's her hair...Maybe it's her stare
Maybe it's her walk...Maybe it's her talk
Maybe it's her kiss...Only I'll know this
Maybe it's her voice...I'm sure glad she's my choice.
Maybe it's her smarts...Whatever it is, I'm glad that we are
In each others' hearts!

Be With Me

Caress me about the shoulders as does an umbrella shades the sun from one who sits on a serene beach. Break the silence and begin conversation as does the first squeal and then cry of a new born baby.

Show me your bright shining smile. Let it beacon as does the burst of sparks and flames ignited in the fireworks display on a still New Year's Evening.

Excite me with your presence. Create a rumble of emotions as did the San Francisco earthquake shake and disfigure noted architecture.

Comfort me as you would pack your most delicate Chinaware to be placed in the care of total strangers. Please don't ever leave me or my tears would forever flow down my cheeks as does the white flushing waters of the Niagara Falls.

The Eyes Have It

Let me look into the eyes of you...I will tell
what I see so true.

I see a love of a special kind...I can even read
your mind.

On your mind is me in your arms...You are
filling me with your charm.

In your arms I would love to forever dwell...
Your feelings are mutual, I can tell.

I know that if your eyes ever blink...That will
never change the way you think.

Please don't ever close your eyes...I'm afraid
our love just might die.

To keep your eyes open, support I'll be happy
to give...I just want this present feeling
and vision to *forever* live!

Our Love

As we drive down the highway to the ice
cream store...I can't help but to notice the
peaceful seashore. The birds fly high above
our heads...I wonder if we should go to the
beach instead!

We continued for ice cream...We sat down in
an atmosphere so serene. We each had a
sundae with a cherry on top...He began to
sing softly to me and I pleaded with him to not
stop.

My heart became filled then over me came a
chill. To control myself I tried...I could not
help but to cry. He asked "What is wrong?"...I
replied, "It's that touching song." It really
spoke about the love issue...To wipe my eyes,
I then needed a tissue.

He took the tissue and wiped my face...I told
him now, "I need your warm embrace." He
asked if I would be his wife...I said, "Sure, if
you promise for life." I again thought about
the birds above...I was still feeling good about
our special and promising love.

Japan

Fresh out of high school, I was blessed, fortunate, special or just lucky to receive A scholarship to Japan...At the time, all I knew was that it was a foreign land.

In America, we call it "Over seas"...At the time, I knew that Japan was famous for its bonsai trees. Before I went to Japan, the language I was eager to speak...Preparation time came by so fast it seemed like only a week.

The airline flight time was fourteen hours...I could barely wait to jump in the shower. When I arrived, I was met with loud Cheers...Within minutes, I took control and eliminated my fears.

From the airport I took the bus...To say "Good morning", I say "Ohayoo-go-zaimus." Japan has a different time zone...To say "Hello", we say "Moshi Moshi" on the telephone.

In a short time, let's say two or three Weeks... I considered myself almost Japanese! I heard and understood...Some people told me that my vocabulary was very good.

I almost mastered the culture, customs and traditions...To my host family, I was a natural addition. To say goodbye, but I'll see you again we say "Genki dei"...Time went by so fast, before I knew it, heading home, I was on my way.

Now at home, my memorabilia is placed neatly in a stack, when I hear the word Japan; boy, I can't wait to go back!

Deliver This Letter...The Sooner The Better

Dear Letter Carrier,

Please deliver this letter. I just want to see if my auntie is feeling better.

For about a month she's been feeling ill. I hope she followed the doctor's orders...And took her daily pill.

I would call her at home...But poor auntie has no phone.

I hope that when she gets my letter, she'll respond right away...In the meantime, I will look to God and pray.

Auntie Sue

I just received a letter from Auntie Sue...
She reported to me that she was feeling kind of
blue.

She complained about pain in her arm, chest
and back...She was relieved when the doctor said
it was not a heart attack.

She said that she was elated to know I
cared...She was even happier to hear that I went
to God in prayer.

The Lost Boss

Bus driver, bus driver, please let me off at my stop. If I had to walk another block...I would just drop. I am so tired from working all day...My boss had a nerve to ask me to stay. I said "no way, I must right now leave"...He began to grab my sleeve.

I told him I was tired and didn't feel well...He said just looking at you I can't tell. My boss said, "If you claim to be so tired...And want to leave...you're fired!"

So I left his workplace...with anger and disappointment on my face.

Bus driver, bus driver, when I get home...I will need to use the telephone.

I will call my former employer...I will let him know that I've contacted my lawyer.

We will initiate a law suit...Just for him trying to be cute!

He will learn to treat people with respect...The Judge will make him issue me a big fat check!

White Wash

In 1993 I wrote a book. Because of racism, it was
dismissed. The name of the book is "Oh, I didn't even
think about this..." It's a wedding planning guide...I wrote
this book with pride. Because the style of the book was
new...I attempted to get a book review.

The story I'm about to tell you is true...I contacted a
magazine called Florist Review. I mail-expressed to them
a copy of the manuscript...I tell you, Marge Nichols
Sullivan is a trip! Initially, to her the subject was of
interest...The final analysis, she proved herself a racist.
She claims that my story was not what they would
include... Now she was being very rude.

She said that I had a nice and interesting story...but she
was only being consistent, with the magazine's history. I
alluded to the fact that I was black...And I think that was
what made her send the transcript back! I asked her if it
could be included in future editions, she said, "Maybe, if
we have space"...Now that was a slap in the face! As
editor the magazine could be as small or large as she
wants...but it's her bigotry she chose to flaunt! I feel
within this poem for this experience I bring closure...To
the world, about the person and magazine I wish to
provide exposure!

After all these years one would think that attitudes have
changed...But no, we are still cursed with people like
this... so deranged! To the arrogant editor, to you I must
tell...Change your ways or you will rot in hell!

In The Mirror

Being in business is not easy...Some people
you meet are sure "sleazy." People dressed
in a blue or white collar...Will do almost
anything for a dollar.

They'll tell you stories, and you know they're
not true... They will then smile at you like
you're a fool! They'll ask to borrow a few
dollars because their car just broke
down...They claim they'll pay you, when they
come back around.

But, of course, you never see them again
ever...You then tell yourself, "I should have
Known better."

Later you meet someone else who claims to
be starving and needs to be fed...But looking
at them, you know the story...So to yourself,
you shake your head.

A bit skeptical but sensitive you reach in you
pocket for some dollars, two or perhaps
three...Then you say to yourself, "That poor
lady, But for the grace of God, it could be
me!"

Illusion

After I boarded the Amtrak...I sat in my seat
and reclined my chair back.

I waited for the conductor to collect my ticket
to ride...My weary and tired demeanor I tried
to hide.

Before I knew it, the train pulled off...The
dryness in my throat caused me to frantically
cough.

I asked the attendant for some water to
drink...He acknowledged my request with a
nod and then a wink. The water quenched
my thirst...Pillows and blankets were handed
out and what do you know, I was first.

Soon I shut my eyes and propped up my
feet...Before I knew it, I was fast asleep.

I felt a lot of motion...and then heard a lot or
commotion. I began to panic and let out a
loud scream...I immediately awoke to find
It was all just a dream!

No Male For Sale

You look at me, why do you stare? Oh no!
Don't you even dare. I can imagine what
You're thinking about...I see the way you're
Checking me out.

I know I'm big, strong, and beautiful. This I'm
Sure you already know. I now have my
Self-respect and dignity...Unlike what
Happened back in history.

I am now my own boss...So you can go get
Loss. I am an independent, healthy, wise,
And strong black male...and no, I am *not* for
Sale.

The Entertaining Barbers

I know some barbers Who are great at what they do...They cut hairstyles both old and new. They can make designs of names and flowers...they're real good but they take hours and hours. While one will cut my hair...The others will take their break and stare. There are some things that slows them down...Most of the time they're busy fooling around. In between conversations, dancing to the music, talking on the telephone or looking at the TV...It sure has me wondering, if my barber has forgotten about me.

Soon he'll come back to me to cut some more...I'll look at the little progress, at the small amount of hair on the floor. I begin wondering what is taking him so long...At that point, he will begin singing a song. He can't seem to just sing to himself...He feels that he has to stop to sing to someone else! After a while has passed...He will begin cleaning me up real fast. He smiles for the experience that was fun...I'll smile and say to myself, "It's about time he's done!" I say "Good job. Oh! don't forget your apron clip...And you may keep the change for a tip."

Silent Prayer

Dear Lord,

I now come to You...with not many requests but only a few.

One, I ask that you bless me to always praise Thee.

Two, please give my parents wisdom as they raise me.

Three, make me always love my neighbor.

Four, make me always know that You are my savior.

And Lord, I thought the requests numbered only four, but I have just one more...

Life eternal is number five...I know eternal life is not easy, it is something for which I must strive.

The Honorable Love

God's Ten Commandments are His greatest
commands...In seven days He made the sky, sea,
and land. He ordered us to honor our father and
mother...God said besides Him, there is none
other.

We know that we shall not kill...When we pray we
must say Lord, if it's Thy will. Jesus said we
should love our neighbor...On the seventh day,
God rested from all His labor.

Jesus is the light of the world...He loves every
man, woman, boy and girl. If you sin, God is
ready to forgive...A long life He wants you to live.

So let's just try to do your best...Leave it to Jesus
and He'll do the rest. Jesus Christ is God's only
son...The Father, Son and Holy Ghost are one.

When you're lonely, look to God above...Only He
can give you everlasting love.

Guide Me

Lord, please keep me humble...Without You, I
know I will stumble.

I don't want to brag or boast...I know I need
You most.

Without you I will moan...Just don't leave me
all alone.

Let me know You're with me, please hold my
hand...When I'm weary, lift me up and let me
stand.

Bless me to always do Your will...My fervent
prayer, I know You'll fulfill.

Bless me when my back is against the wall...
I need You, oh Lord, I need You to hear my
call.

Patience

Lord, please give me patience...I enjoy my clear conscience.

I don't want to say or do the wrong thing...God knows I don't want to swing.

I don't want to hit the wrong man...Because before a judge, I will have to stand.

If so, guilty, I might be found...So Lord, let my thoughts and actions be sound.

What Must A Man Do?

A man is a male of the human race...He is expected to
speak in a tone of bass. A popular name for a man is
Dave...Most men dread their daily shave. Most men are
lovers of sports...On Fathers' Day many will receive
wacky-pattern boxer shorts. By the age of forty many
men will lose their hair...The site of a pretty woman will
definitely elicit a stare. Many men feel it's their obligation
to fight...If in the presence of a crowd, they'll want to show
off their might. Some men feel that a man is not suppose
to cry...To tell you the truth some wouldn't know how,
even if they tried.

Some men are ashamed to be in church, they don't want
their friends to see...I say to them, be bold, you're in
God's army. Some might visit a church and be somewhat
amazed...I encourage them to sing, shout and give God
the praise! If a woman in the church smiles at them, they
might see this as a tease...They are really insulted when
asked to pray and fall on their knees.

Some feel that certain functions in the church are female
roles...If they join in God will save their souls. So I issue
a challenge to all males who are real men...I'll say this
once and not again. Join right in and do what's right...Lift
up the name of Jesus Christ. You come to church, not to
search for a wife...But you come that you may have
eternal life!

A Real Man

A real man is a male who can show his
love...Pure and gentle like a dove.

A real man is a male who is not ashamed to
cry...One who knows that to beat a failure is
to try.

A real man is a male who is not afraid to
show his pain...He is one who does for others
with no plans for personal gain.

A real man is a male who sticks in there
through thick And thin...He's one who's not too
big to repent for his sins.

A real man is a male who's not ashamed of
his meekness...And who doesn't see this as a
weakness.

A real man is a male who will be bold for
Christ...He's one who will not forget that for
eternal life Jesus paid the price!

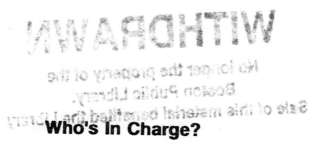

Who's In Charge?

Dear Lord,

You have recently displayed Your power in an earthquake...You said the word and the earth did shake. You showed the world that You are the boss...You showed us that all of our mortal possessions and in some cases, lives could easily be a total loss.

You further showed us what You could do... we know that all Your powers are nothing new. For the rest of us who didn't perish, Your precious name we will cherish.

Please continue to extend Your loving arm of protection...Bless us with the will to follow Your direction. Lord, all things You do are great...I want to walk that path that's narrow and straight.
You don't need to show me Your work for me to be amazed...Because I already know Your powers, I just want to always give You the praise!

114

Lord, Please Walk With Me

As I leave, Lord please bless my home...The
dangerous streets I'm about to roam.

Watch over me as I cross the streets...Me in
Your arms, I pray you'll keep.

I realize that out there is rampant crime...I ask
that You guide me each and every time.

To my home I wish to return...How to give
You more praises, I wish to learn.

Again, I ask that You keep my home intact...
And Lord, please bless me to safely make it
back.